Inventing Computers

by Racquel Foran

FOCUS
READERS.

BEACON

www.focusreaders.com

Focus Readers is distributed by North Star Editions:
sales@northstareditions.com | 888-417-0195

Produced for Focus Readers by Red Line Editorial.

Photographs ©: Shutterstock Images, cover, 1, 4, 6, 8, 13, 14–15, 16, 19, 21, 22, 25, 27, 29; Reading Room 2020/Alamy, 11

Library of Congress Cataloging-in-Publication Data
Names: Foran, Racquel, 1966- author.
Title: Inventing computers / by Racquel Foran.
Description: Lake Elmo, MN : Focus Readers, [2022] | Series: Amazing inventions | Includes index. | Audience: Grades 2-3
Identifiers: LCCN 2021041726 (print) | LCCN 2021041727 (ebook) | ISBN 9781637390450 (hardcover) | ISBN 9781637390993 (paperback) | ISBN 9781637391532 (ebook) | ISBN 9781637392041 (pdf)
Subjects: LCSH: Computers--Juvenile literature. | Computers--History--Juvenile literature.
Classification: LCC QA76.23 .F667 2022 (print) | LCC QA76.23 (ebook) | DDC 004.09--dc23
LC record available at https://lccn.loc.gov/2021041726
LC ebook record available at https://lccn.loc.gov/2021041727

Printed in the United States of America
Mankato, MN
012022

About the Author

Racquel Foran is a freelance writer from British Columbia, Canada. She is the author of several books for school-age readers on a variety of topics. When she isn't writing, Foran enjoys tending to her Little Free Library, painting, and walking her dogs by the river.

Table of Contents

Chapter 1

Simple Shopping

A girl and her mom enter a shopping mall. They want to buy rain boots. So, they find a touch screen map near the door. It shows them where to find a shoe store.

 People can tap a touch screen map to get directions.

 Many stores and restaurants use tablets to take payments. A tablet is a type of computer.

Inside the store, the clerk scans a **barcode** on the shoebox. The price of the boots shows on a screen.

The girl's mom uses her credit card to pay. She signs her name on the screen. Then, she taps a button to get an email **receipt**.

All these things happen with the help of computers. Computers are machines that store and process **data**. They come in many sizes. And they often send information to other devices.

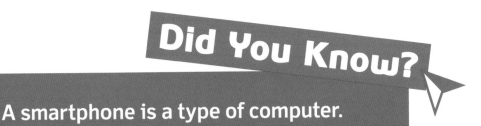

Did You Know?

A smartphone is a type of computer.

Chapter 2

History of Computers

People created the first computers in the late 1800s. These machines did simple **calculations**. Early computers used punch cards. Each punch card had holes in it. People slid these cards into a machine.

 Many computers are based on counting machines invented by Charles Babbage.

The holes were a code. They told the machine what to do. For example, they could help the machine count large numbers.

In the 1940s, computers began using vacuum tubes. Vacuum tubes acted like tiny switches. They could stop or send electric

Did You Know?

In 1801, Joseph-Marie Jacquard made a loom that used punch cards. The holes told the loom what pattern to weave.

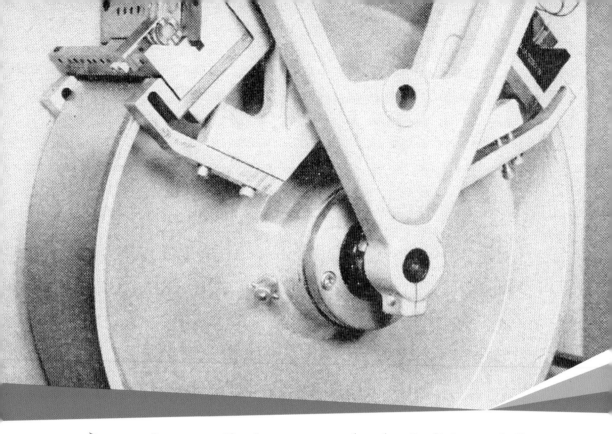

> A magnetic drum spun slowly. As it turned, the computer made marks on its surface.

signals. This helped the computer process information. Computers used magnetic drums for memory. These parts could record and store information.

Transistors were invented in 1947. Computers could use them instead of vacuum tubes. Transistors worked faster. They used less energy. They were much smaller, too. As a result, computers became faster and smaller.

In the 1960s, computers began using **integrated circuits**. One

Did You Know?

Computers began to have keyboards and **monitors** in the 1960s.

 Microchips helped computers become smaller and do more tasks.

circuit could hold thousands of

transistors. But it took up very little

space. So, it was sometimes called

a microchip. Thanks to microchips,

computers became much more

powerful. They also cost less to

make. More people could buy them.

ENIAC

ENIAC was one of the first electronic computers. It was built in 1946. Like many early computers, ENIAC was big and heavy. It weighed 30 tons (27 metric tons). And it filled an entire room. It was 50 feet (15 m) long and 30 feet (9.1 m) wide.

ENIAC used more than 17,000 vacuum tubes. It could do 5,000 calculations every second. The US military used it to make charts. It found how far bullets and bombs could fly. Before, people did this math by hand. Today, one microchip can do even more work more quickly.

To give ENIAC instructions, people had to plug in or unplug many wires.

Chapter 3

How Computers Work

Computers have many parts. The physical parts are called hardware. They include the screen, keyboard, and **hard drive**. Software tells these parts what to do. To create software, people write code.

 A computer's cables and circuits are part of its hardware. So is the case that surrounds them.

Code is a set of instructions. It tells a computer how to do a task, one step at a time.

Computers do many different kinds of tasks. They take in data. This task is called input. Computers store and process data. They also output data. That means they show or send information.

For example, teachers use computers to make report cards. First, they type students' test scores. A computer saves these

Parts and Processes

Computers use different parts and devices to do different tasks.

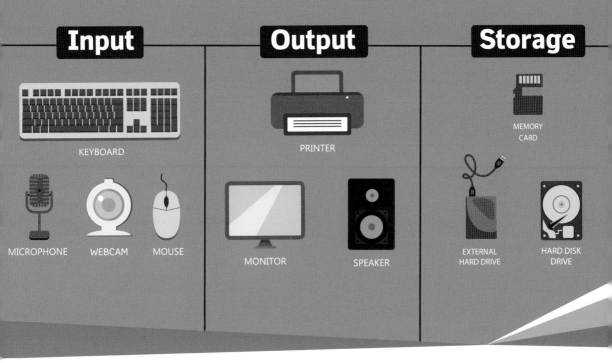

Input — KEYBOARD, MICROPHONE, WEBCAM, MOUSE

Output — PRINTER, MONITOR, SPEAKER

Storage — MEMORY CARD, EXTERNAL HARD DRIVE, HARD DISK DRIVE

numbers in its memory. It uses them to find each student's grade. This grade shows on the screen. Teachers can also print grades.

Networks connect computers together. These computers can send and receive information. Some networks have just a few computers. Other networks are huge. For example, the internet connects millions of computers around the world. Code tells them where and how to find information.

Did You Know?

Some servers work in huge groups. They fill entire rooms or buildings.

 Data centers use big groups of servers to send and store information.

Servers help, too. These computers send information where it needs to go.

Computers also work with other devices. For example, they control many **appliances**. They help these devices track, sense, and send information.

Chapter 4

How Computers Help

Computers make many tasks faster and easier. In the past, people did calculations by hand. They also kept records on paper. These tasks could take lots of time and effort. So could finding information.

 People can use computers to learn, write, play games, and much more.

Computers can store huge amounts of data. They keep it organized. And they can find information quickly.

Early computers were big and expensive. Many were also hard to use. Very few people had access to them. Today, computers are almost everywhere. People use them at work, at home, and on the go.

In fact, computers now do many tasks **automatically**. Many factories use machines that are controlled by computers. Code tells the machines

 Robots on assembly lines help put together cars.

how to build, mix, and package products. These machines are much faster than human workers.

Many newer computers use artificial intelligence (AI). AI does not need instructions from humans.

Instead, a computer or program uses information stored in its memory to learn on its own.

For example, one AI looked at many pictures. It learned to identify different types of animals. Some cities use AI to control traffic. The AI learns what times of day have the busiest traffic. Then it adjusts

Did You Know?

Some AIs can translate. They change words from one language into another.

 AI is involved in choosing what people see on social media.

the timing of the stoplights. As people continue to invent new programs and devices, computers may help do even more tasks.

FOCUS ON
Inventing Computers

Write your answers on a separate piece of paper.

1. Write a few sentences describing what AI is and how it works.

2. What is one way your life would be different if computers didn't exist?

3. When were integrated circuits invented?
   - **A.** in the late 1800s
   - **B.** in the 1940s
   - **C.** in the 1960s

4. Which is an example of input?
   - **A.** A computer's speaker plays music.
   - **B.** A computer shows words on its screen.
   - **C.** A person types words using a computer's keyboard.

5. What does **memory** mean in this book?

*Computers used magnetic drums for **memory**. These parts could record and store information.*

    A. a way of deleting information forever

    B. a way of keeping information to use later

    C. a part of a person's brain

6. What does **physical** mean in this book?

*The **physical** parts are called hardware. They include the screen, keyboard, and hard drive.*

    A. able to be touched or held

    B. able to be made with code

    C. made up or not real

Answer key on page 32.

Glossary

appliances
Machines that have specific jobs, such as stoves or fans.

automatically
Done on its own, without any outside control.

barcode
A series of lines that a machine can read to get information.

calculations
Math done to find an answer or solve a problem.

data
Information collected to study or track something.

hard drive
The part of a computer that stores information.

integrated circuits
Small flat boards on which many tiny electronic devices, such as transistors, are connected together.

monitors
Screens that show images made by computers.

receipt
A paper or message showing that a person has bought something.

transistors
Devices that control the flow of electricity by turning on or off.

To Learn More

BOOKS

Berg, Shannon. *Before Computers*. Lake Elmo, MN: Focus Readers, 2020.

Dickmann, Nancy. *How Computers Work*. New York: Gareth Stevens Publishing, 2020.

Smibert, Angie. *Inside Computers*. Minneapolis: Abdo Publishing, 2019.

NOTE TO EDUCATORS

Visit **www.focusreaders.com** to find lesson plans, activities, links, and other resources related to this title.

Index

Answer Key: 1. Answers will vary; **2.** Answers will vary; **3.** C; **4.** C; **5.** B; **6.** A